Train Your Dog in Seconds

Kevin "The Dog Tutor" Meehan

PublishAmerica
Baltimore

© 2004 by Kevin Meehan.

All rights reserved. No part of this book may be reproduced, stored in a retrieval system or transmitted in any form or by any means without the prior written permission of the publishers, except by a reviewer who may quote brief passages in a review to be printed in a newspaper, magazine or journal.

First printing

ISBN: 1-4137-2790-5
PUBLISHED BY PUBLISHAMERICA, LLLP
www.publishamerica.com
Baltimore

Printed in the United States of America

*I dedicate this book to my Mom,
for always cheering me on
and encouraging me to believe
in the unbelievable.*

Dogs are absolutely amazing. As you know they can guide humans who are blind, they can sniff out contraband and bombs, they can automatically try to protect us without our asking, they will go get something for you so you don't have to get up, and they are everybody's buddy.

I have seen a dog walk a 6 foot tight rope (cable) and I have also seen a dog walking on its hind legs while balancing a glass of coca-cola on it's snout. I am sure you know of or have heard or seen something amazing involving a dog. Believe in their potential.

— They are super-adaptive animals —

Table of Contents

Introduction: Think About This..7
    A Dog Named Chance..13
        (A Rescue Story)

The 4 Key Ways to a Great Dog...16
    1) Train in Seconds...16
    2) Training Without Training — 5 Word Sequence.........18
    3) Sub-Sonic Training..23
    4) Lifestyle Training..24

Specific Five Word Command Instructions........................26

    Sit..26
    Stay...27
    Down..28
    Come...29
    Heel (Or Anti-Pull)..31

Puppies...37
    24 Hours to House Train...38
    Building Confidence...39
    Mine/Yours...39
    "No" and "Drop"..40
    Correction/Punishment...44
    Why and How of Chokers...46

Protection Training..48

Summary..50

— Dogs are constant optimists —

Introduction

Think about this

Take the time to look around you and you'll see how deeply dogs are immersed in North American society. They're everywhere. Not just in your neighbourhood or city, but they appear in TV commercials and sitcoms, movies (with starring roles), billboard ads, magazines, gift cards, key chains, books, calendars, and even cemeteries. The list is exhaustive. I think you'd be hard pressed to find anyone who isn't a dog lover. We put their pictures on our walls or night tables. We buy them birthday and Christmas gifts. We dress them up (sometimes embarrassingly so). We brush their teeth. We let them sleep in our beds and lick our faces.

Why do we love dogs so much? It's simple: who else would love us as unconditionally as good ol' Fido? A dog won't lecture, nag, judge, reject, or abandon you. They have that uncanny sixth sense; they can tune in to how you're feeling…and respond in exactly the right way. Dogs can understand over 100 words or signals (this manual teaches seven), so it's relatively easy to communicate with them.
I never apply any teaching or training that is simply for the convenience of man, and I will never recommend any. My objectives are always for the convenience and nurturing of the dog. A puppy is comparable to having a baby, and a dog is comparable to having a child. You wouldn't lock your child in a cage for eight to ten hours a day, buzz it electronically, or put a strap across its face and inflict a little pressure when you go for walks. If you love your dog then you will love this book; it illustrates how easy and convenient it is to have a great dog.

In the years that I have been working with and training dogs, I have discovered a system that is simple, easy to use, and works with any dog and any owner. *Train Your Dog in Seconds* will allow you to train your dog in a loving, gentle way.

Imagine if you were the first and only person to ever have a dog in the world. How would you know what to do? You should start by not letting it of your sight. Your close observation would prevent any wrong behaviour. You should also speak to it one word at a time and look for signs of understanding. These are the two primary methods for successful dog training: constant observation and one word/one second training sessions.

Constant observation will result in little correction, while one word training sessions will program the dog's mind to naturally co-operate and be successful. Your dog should always get a loving pat or a kind and perky response (good girl! good boy!) when he or she obeys any command. This will please your dog immensely; after all, his primary objective is to make you happy. His pride and confidence will increase, not much different from humans getting a "pat on the back" for a job well done, although Fido should receive twenty, thirty, or forty of these a day. Of course, it's impossible to train a dog without ever giving it negative attention, especially during the puppy months. There will be times when your dog pushes your patience, disappoints you, or even makes you angry. Try to remain calm — remember, your dog is like your child, and should be treated with the same high morals. *Never stop the kind encouragement!* Even years from now continue to give lots of daily encouragement.

I want you to be like a dog. YOU join the dog. Show interest in their world. Remember to give your dog some freedom on walks. Don't make the entire walk to your needs. After all, we are walking for the dog, aren't we? Get the dog to participate (in whichever activity) and then follow or let the dog lead on or off the leash (depending on control). Go lie with them when they are laying down, run with them when they run, join them when they go swimming or exploring ... show some interest in the scents they find by stopping and letting nature be itself ... there are plenty of ways to GO to their world and really become friends who will bond quickly on a foundation of trust and respect. JOIN your dog at least once a day and you will both enjoy it. This will cement your friendship and create a bond based on a foundation of trust and respect.

Most dog owners want a well-behaved pet, not a competition dog! Nor do they want a dog conditioned to behave according to a particular circumstance, such as a setting, a leash, a treat, a ball, or whatever the stimulus may be. If your goal is to have a perfectly trained dog like the ones on TV and in movies, forget about it. These dogs are "weird" dogs subjected to hours of intense training. Many can't walk down a city street, or be off leash other than when playing "the game." They may be so dysfunctional that they must be crated when not performing. Do you really want obsessive-compulsive disorder in your family pet? Or do you want a great dog-park dog? This book will teach you how to communicate effectively with your dog. Your dog will learn to look to you for leadership and direction, and you will learn how to provide the leadership and direction that all dogs need, in a "language" your dog will intuitively understand. The communication method I use in *Train Your Dog in Seconds* is the quickest and easiest method that I have ever seen. Think about this for a moment, most of us believe we humans are the superior beings ... but are we really? A dog has a greater threshold for pain, temperature extremes, and chance of surviving should "The Bomb" ever hit. A dog will also outperform us at running, jumping, hearing, smelling, and seeing. Dogs also have that extra sense that we can't explain ... like knowing when you are coming home just before you arrive, or knowing someone has bad intentions. They can be sensitive to your mood, or get excited every time you leave or go out — except when you go to work in the morning, and many other unexplained sensory workings.

— Treat your dog more like a human —

The Top Twelve Rules for a Well-behaved Dog

Never scold your dog when he comes to you — go to him if he needs correction.

Don't point at your dog's face.

Don't get your dog excited without reason. Keep him calm.

Avoid standing over your dog.

Never shout at your dog. Use a deep, low, and slow voice when reprimanding.

Never strike your dog.

Do not use "nose-strap" devices, pronged collars, or electronic devices.

No roughhousing.

No teasing. (Some people think this is playing.)

Never disrupt your dog when he's content. (That is, unless you're going for a walk or some other significant reason.)

Move slowly to correct your dog. Quick movement will disrupt him before you can get to him.

Be 100% consistent and observant.

— Dogs are always ready, willing, and able
to do just about anything
you could want to do, and
they are ready in seconds —

A Dog Named Chance

A Rescue Story

There are beautiful dogs out there, and then there's Chance. But this female German shepherd wasn't always in such great shape. At only ten months of age her former owners abandoned her, and she was found by the side of the road and brought to a nearby vet. She had an intestinal infection, and it would cost approximately $1000 to fix her up and keep her in the hospital for a week or more. The good Samaritans who found her paid the bill, with absolutely no intentions of keeping her, and then dropped her off at the S.P.C.A. for the second time in her short life. She was a bolter, a leash puller, and possibly a biter. Judging by the way she cowered, I assumed she had been hit or beaten. She obviously had no training, and it seemed as though she had been left outdoors.

Her cowering was so bad that the first time I opened the door to our new home together, she refused to come in. Nothing would make her enter the house, not even soft-spoken words of encouragement. She would cower at all times. I had never seen anything like it.

Months later, Chance and I drove an hour away to visit the vet who saved her life. I wanted to show him how strong, healthy, and happy she was. Ironically, one of the people who found her was soon coming. When Mr. Smith arrived, he did a double take upon seeing Chance. He couldn't believe it was her...he was so happy and relieved. He had wanted to take her, but he already owned three dogs. Lucky for me, and for Chance.

Despite all of the mistreatment that must have happened to her (and I cringe to think about it), Chance is now completely rebuilt physically and emotionally. She is an outstanding success story, and the techniques and methods found in this book are responsible. Chance received praise for so many little accomplishments and successes that she believed in herself once again. In only three months of applying the 4 key ways, Chance now sits, stays, downs, comes, and heels off leash. She obeys four different come-type commands, retrieves, and politely sits by the door to go out. She has never messed in the house, sleeps on her own sleeping bag-bed on the floor at the foot of my bed, loves people, loves other dogs, is very attentive to children, jumps on command onto 3-4 foot heights or more, guards at night, and understands the word "no!" In short, I can take her anywhere and she is always a pleasure to have as my companion. In these three months, I have never applied an official "training session." I coached her in seconds, and you can too!

— Humans are dogs' best friends —

The 4 Key Ways to a Great Dog

The best opportunity to start training is when your dog is young, ideally about eight to ten weeks old. A dog is almost as mentally competent as it will ever be at about twelve weeks. For those who have an older dog, the method may take longer. Older dogs may need to unlearn some bad behaviours (refuting the old adage that you can't teach an old dog new tricks). Young pups may not be as clever as an adult dog, but they are easily manipulated, quite predictable, and easier to teach and lead. Similar to a small child, puppies must be constantly protected and taught the right behaviours.

The 4 Key Ways are meant to be understood and applied in combination.

Key Way #1: Train in Seconds

Using One Second Training sessions will almost "program" your dog to success and will lead to an amazing subconscious cooperation in your dog or pup. You can probably find examples of how your dog has been "naturally" trained in just seconds. This ability is not unique to only me, a qualified dog trainer. For example, an owner opens the drawer at the bottom of the stove and his dog comes over to investigate. His collar tags get caught up in the handle, and the owner frees him within seconds. To this day the dog avoids the stove at all costs. Or how about an owner who never lets her dog on her bed, but decides one morning to invite the dog up for a few minutes of cuddling. Later that evening, as the owner crawls into bed for the night, the dog immediately jumps up with her. He was invited only once and he suddenly feels welcome any time! The owner quickly removes him and gives a stern, "No!" The dog no longer jumps on the bed and the owner does not invite.

In most cases a dog needs to learn just once (or once a day or once per session). It can learn in just seconds! Believe it! If your dog is awake, it is being trained, and the best form of training teaches the dog as quickly as possible with the least amount of correction.

As you start to teach your pup the word commands all dogs need to know, limit them to one-second time intervals (sitting for one second, staying for one second, and so on). I want you to have many, many short successful moments throughout your day. Later on, you will increase the time lapses by a few seconds each time. Eventually your dog will sit, stay, down, or heel indefinitely.

Doors – An Example Of a Daily Routine Opportunity

Dogs are always trying to figure out how to get what they want from us. Doors are a perfect example. All dogs want us to open the door so they can go outside. The following routine is very effective for getting your dog to wait by the door in an appropriate manner (as opposed to scratching and whining at the door).

Only open the door if Fido is sitting there quietly. If Fido is very young (eight to ten weeks), place him in front of the door then pause before opening it. Open the door slowly. At this tender age don't worry about being too strict with this routine; let the dog work at its own pace. When it is able to sit for two to three seconds, open the door quickly. Increase the time to four to five seconds, and so on, week by week. (This "sit" also implies a "stay," but do not use the "stay" command. It comes later and is a separate command altogether.)

Soon Fido will be quietly waiting by the door when he wants to go outside. By this time he has been *imprinted*, and waiting by the door is as natural as eating. It's up to you to maintain this in your dog's mind, by observing him closely and being sure to open the door when he wants outside. Training in seconds is really about changing your consciousness to communicate in a way your dog can recognize. You will soon realize that your dog is almost automatically adaptable. Let him think it was his idea.

Key Way #2: Training Without Training

This method has been partly explained in Key Way #1. By using every part of your everyday interaction with your dog as a development routine, *your dog learns good behaviour as his only behaviour.* His own activity periods are a good time to teach. Always remember, "If your dog is awake it is being trained."

Training Without Training is a dissection of what a dog needs to know, and then spoon feeding it to him slowly, one step at a time, one second at a time. Owners and others in the household often make the mistake of teaching Fido to sit, stay, down, come, stop, no, off, and so on, each using different techniques, different voice tones, and during different activities, all in the same day. The following routine is as far as I go in terms of any formal training sessions to quickly teach a dog the most common commands. Do it for ten seconds at a time (or longer, it's up to you). In the weeks to come you will have this 10 second routine down pat and should apply it every day as often as you can.

Five Word Sequence

Sit, stay, down, come, and heel are the five words best used to begin training your dog. Specific instructions for teaching each of these commands can be found in later pages and should be reviewed before beginning this sequence.

Day 1 – Sit

First you need to confirm that your dog knows the "sit" word. This may seem too simple or boring, but it is critical to master; it is the foundation for the rest of the words/commands. Say "sit" to Fido over a one- to two-hour period while playing, walking, or whenever the opportunity arises. Say it only once. Do this sixty times for one to two seconds each, always followed by a generous reward. It's up to you what goes on in between "sit," but don't use other commands or use failure correction. Try to command "sit" when you are fairly confident your dog *will* sit. If you don't get the right response, turn away, and carry on with what you were doing. Wait a minute and try again.

Day 2 – Stay (sit and stay)

Two to three days later, you can begin the "stay" command. Start with "sit" as in day one, to confirm the previous lesson to yourself and to your dog (five to ten successful sit commands should do). Using the "stay" instructions on the following pages, first command "sit," then command "stay." Hold the stay posture for five seconds. Reward proudly, when the routine is over. Repeat sixty times over the same training period as day one. Over the next week and following weeks increase the "stay" time by five seconds every day.

Day 3 – Down (sit, stay, down)

Begin this lesson with a few "sit" commands, followed by a few "sit and stay" commands, followed by the "down" command (from the "sit and stay" position). Once your dog is in the "down" position for a few seconds, reward proudly; the routine is over. Repeat "sit, stay, down" sequence sixty times over the same time period as days one and two. As time goes on, increase the "down" time by five seconds a day.

Day 4 – Come (sit, stay, down, come)

Again, begin this lesson with the "sit" command, then the "sit and stay," the "sit, stay, down," then "come." In the "down" position, walk backwards five to ten feet away from your dog and command "come." Reward proudly as the routine is over. Repeat the sequence sixty times over the same period as days one, two, and three. Over time walk farther and farther away before you command "come."

Day 5 – Heel (sit, stay, down, come, heel)

Use the same routine again, starting with a few "sit" commands, then "sit and stay," then "sit, stay, and down," then "sit, stay, down, come," and then "heel." As your dog comes, quickly move him to the heel position and start walking (ten to twenty feet). Reward proudly when the routine is over. When first introducing this part, you don't have to be strict with the correct heel as much as you should be sending the message of, "Behave! We are walking." Repeat sixty times over the same period as days one, two, three, and four. After a few days of this, start to increase your standards for heeling, and follow the heel instructions to a tee. As Fido comes to you, encourage him to walk around behind you to the heel position beside you.

Once you master this five word sequence, you will find many opportunities to repeat it or parts of it throughout your day. Eventually your dog will respond to any of these words individually. Remember to always reward Fido for responding correctly to any word command, even after he is perfectly trained, which could be years later. Randomly training without training will never take any really valuable time out of your day (once you are fluent with the sequence).

This method stimulates the dog's sequential thinking patterns (what comes next). I have noticed that dogs trained in this manner will mature quicker and are easier to manage. Dogs rely heavily on their sequential thinking ability, so delivering these words in this order, which also requires an action from the dog, capitalizes on its natural ability to anticipate what's coming. The commands' connecting pattern link the behaviours together to perform the routine. The reward comes not after every word command but after every *last* word command.

Rewards during these initial lessons of training without training should consist primarily of lots of love, excitement, and touching. Eventually this can be toned down to "good girl, good boy" or whatever you like.

In summary, Training Without Training constantly uses your time with your dog as behaviour adjustment. It requires consistency and constant observation. It is a kindergarten classroom no matter how big and fierce the dog is.

— Your dog wants to be involved in every second of your life —

Key Way #3: Sub-Sonic Training

Sub-Sonic Training refers to reaching a dog on a very deep level, subconsciously and emotionally. This is done through voice control, keeping your voice low and deep, and speaking in a slow manner. I can't tell you how important it is to reach your dog on an emotional level. Just like with humans, anything that affects a dog emotionally tends to stick with him for a period of time. By using a deep and low voice, you will reach your dog emotionally, and leave a serious and lasting impression.

Reaching your dog's subconscious is much easier than you may think. I have already made reference to this in Key Way #1 and Key Way #2. Your dog is being trained subconsciously during the opening of the door routine (found in Key Way #1). To the dog this is just the way it is, the way it always was, and the way it always will be.

Sub-Sonic Training is training without failure. It lets the dog learn the right way to do things from the very beginning. It is both a mental method and a voice correction method. The lower the note in your voice, the deeper the penetration. Think of a dog's growl, which is used to correct or warn another dog. It is low and slow, and all dogs know what it means. It is more serious than a shrill squeal. Through your own low, slow voice, you can have the same effect as the growl. Fido wants nothing more than to please the "big dog" or "leader of the pack" — YOU! Making your dog feel pushed out of the pack when it does something wrong is the quickest way to reach your dog and change his behaviour. Sub-Sonic Training is magic your dog just cannot figure out.

By watching your dog throughout the day, you'll begin to recognize when he is about to engage in bad behaviour: chewing on the table leg, peeing in the house, digging a hole in the lawn, and so on. You will then have the ability to stop him before the bad behaviour occurs. Voice correction in a low, deep voice is your response to bad behaviour.

Understanding Sub-Sonic Training helps link the 4 Key Ways to the most important must-have commands of no, drop, come, stay, and heel (described in detail later).

Key Way #4: Lifestyle Training

Lifestyle Training is a combination of understanding the potential of training in seconds, training without training, and sub-sonic training.

There are many opportunities every day to teach your dog the basic commands of control. Every time you interact with your dog — entering or exiting the house, feeding, going to bed, walking — is an opportunity to teach. If you teach your dog from the beginning to do something *one way,* this is the only behaviour your dog will learn! If you want Fido to sit at the door prior to opening it, then never open it if he is not sitting. Dogs are very cunning and will figure out a way to get you to open that door, so don't slip up! By capitalizing on regular daily life routines, you can train your dog to your own unique lifestyle. Consistency is key. These "lessons" will only last seconds, but there will be many in a regular day, compounded by the days, weeks, and months. Soon you will reach your goal of having a well-behaved dog.

— No matter where you're going, your dog can't wait to get there —

Specific Five Word Command Instructions

Sit, Stay, Down, Come, and Heel

Key Way #2, Training Without Training, introduced you to the five-word command sequence. You may find that Fido is clueless about what these words mean. The following specific techniques for each of the five commands will help Fido to learn these words, thus making your training a little bit easier.

Sit

Early on in this book, I asked you to observe your dog closely, even to join your dog in his activities. You may have noticed that he rarely sat. Most dogs either stand or lay down. For some reason, we humans seem to think it's important to teach this behaviour. I'm not against it, but I do find it a remedial command to teach a dog. I suggest it be used as a prelude to the next command or task.

Treats are the best way to teach "sit." Hold the treat 8-10 inches above your dog's head and slowly move it backwards toward his rear. Command "sit!" The moment he sits, give him the treat immediately (the one-second rule).

A dog's natural biomechanics create the sitting position. As the treat moves backwards, it is natural and easy for a dog to lower his rear end to the ground while the head naturally rises to get closer to the treat.

Gradually increase the intervals between the sit and the treat from one second up to as long as you want – but increase the intervals by one to two seconds at a time.

If Fido fails to respond to this command, you may need to touch him. Place one finger on the center top of his rear end, applying gentle pressure. Don't poke. Increase the pressure until Fido is sitting, while repeating the command, "sit," "sit," "sit." When he complies, reward immediately.

Do not be guilty of impatience! Give Fido three or four seconds response time after the very first command. Speed will come later. Within days, your dog will respond to the sit command instantly — every time!

Teach this command slowly, daily, and with many short routines rather than one long session. Eventually you can use hand or other signals to indicate "sit." Just be sure to keep everything consistent.

Stay

The environment around you and your dog is a very logical setting for teaching "stay." What a perfect opportunity to teach your dog without going out of your way! These exercises can be performed whenever there is a change in environment: inside to outside (or vice versa), in and out of a vehicle, pavement to turf, the start of a walk or game, and so on.

I recommend using a 6-foot leash when beginning this lesson. Walk one step sideways away from your dog. Command "stay," and hold your hand up to block your eyes from Fido's for one to two seconds. Blocking the primary target of observation (your eyes) sends a very distinct message: to "stay" even if you are out of sight. Eventually, you'll be able to command a "stay" from 20 to 40 feet or more by simply holding up your hand sideways in front of you to block your face from Fido's view. Take another two steps away until you reach the end of the leash. After every two-step interval, go back to Fido's side. Offer a love reward or treat for each time he has stayed.

Repeat the above directions one more time, but now try to circle your dog while commanding "stay," if necessary (he may stay without the command). Go back to him with a love reward or treat at least twice before you've made a full circle. Repeat until you can walk a complete circle while he stays (offering a reward at the end). Never say "come" to your dog during these early stages of "stay" training, always go to your dog to reward and end the training session. Soon you will be confident enough to start exercising and testing off leash (I'd recommend a fenced yard to start).

Most importantly, build the dogs sense of security. That is, they are secure that you will always come back for them, and "stay" never hurts. Interestingly, a dog has a difficult time learning "stay" because he is asked to do nothing so don't be surprised if Fido fails. As soon as he gets it right once, presto! He now knows how to "stay."

Down

This is a useful command when you need your dog to stay put and out of the way (in most cases).

The simplest way of teaching the "down" command is with a food treat. From the "sit" position, hold the treat in front of Fido's nose as you move it closer to the ground. As he reaches for the treat, his natural biomechanics cause him to lie down. Once he is in the down position, reward immediately. Like all other commands, a 100% success rate is desired. To achieve this, always train the dog very slowly. Increase the "down" time by only seconds as your confidence builds. He will start to anticipate your actions, and in a short time will lie down before your hand reaches the ground. You can now create a simple hand signal for the same effect.

Don't be guilty of commanding your dog to "down" only when he is bad or when you're in a bad mood. Command "down" to love, to play, to brush, and so on.

You may choose to use "down" to imply "stay" or command "down" then "stay" to "stay-down." You can also say, "Down," or "Lay down," when your dog is already lying down on his own.

Come

The "come" command is probably the most important word to teach. It has also proven to be the most difficult for most people to learn and for dogs to respond. The three techniques offered here always work: 1) The Super-Come Secret, 2) The Invisible Leash, and 3) Come for Nothing. Practice these techniques faithfully, and use all three as often as you can. Remember to *avoid failure*! NEVER have your dog "come" to be scolded!

1) The Super-Come Secret

The next time you go for a walk, take your dog to an open but isolated (no other animals/people) area, or at an off-leash park. I like forest trails. Release your dog from the leash and encourage him to go (if need be). Don't take your eyes off him and wait for him to look back at you — he will. He is more concerned for you than you are for him and will always check on you. He will look at you approximately every ten to thirty seconds. As soon as he looks at you, stop walking. Say, "Good boy," or "Good girl," or something happy and positive. This should go on two to three times (probably in the first minute). The next time he looks at you, command, "Come," once! Act happy and excited. As Fido comes to you, keep saying, "Come, come, come," with more and more excitement and speed until he reaches you. Reward proudly and release.

Don't call your dog to "come" every time he looks at you. Do call him to "come" once every four times he looks at you. The other three times call out, "Good boy," or whatever you choose.

It is important to always stop moving when using the "come" command. This gives your dog a stationary object to come to!

2) The Invisible Leash

You now know that your dog will always look back at you when he's off running around and enjoying himself. It is critical that you always study your dog so that every time he looks at you he gets a cue. He will not run off and disappear. This distance control becomes an invisible leash.

Once you have a certain degree of control, test the invisible leash theory. As your dog is likely running off ahead of you, quickly hide and wait; you have just broken the invisible leash. Fido will be along in twenty seconds or so looking for you, just as you would go looking for him should he break the invisible leash. Occasionally performing this routine will help build the bond between you and your dog. When Fido finds you, this is a very important time for reward (love), and lots of it.

Because you never want your dog to fail, create "winning" situations. Don't let Fido off leash at a crowded carnival and then hide on him! I like the forest because it's easy to tuck behind a tree and watch my dog as it "discovers" I'm gone. Remember, in most cases, when your dog looks directly at you, he is looking for a signal or message. Again, I emphasize to always study your dog until you are fully pleased with his consistent behaviour. By studying your dog, you won't miss the "cues" he gives you. Communicate a lot; dogs live in a world of signals: animal trails, scents, and instinct.

3) Come for Nothing

Come for Nothing is the culmination of the above two techniques. So far you have commanded your dog only at times when you are confident he will come, and you rewarded him justly. On a daily basis it would be easy to give your dog ten, twenty, or thirty of these "come" commands, for example, feeding time, going for a walk, when you come home, and so on. Up until now, I've advised you to reward your dog with either treats or love. I can guarantee that Fido loves to receive both. Although food is a great motivator, you won't always have it on hand, and besides, you want Fido to come to you without a "bribe." In due time, phase out treats as a reward, and only give your love and affection. "Come for nothing" implies instructions to frequently have your dog "come" for no apparent reason (around the house or yard) and/or to say "come" when it is naturally coming to you anyway.

Heel (Or Anti-pull)

A 6-foot leash and choker will be required.

Fido doesn't mean to pull you around; you just walk at a different pace. Dogs are built to travel long distances efficiently with a steady gait. You'd probably get around a little quicker with four legs, too. You can, however, teach your dog to walk at your pace. You may have read in other manuals or guide books that a dog must walk (heel) and stop within a ¼ inch zone. My principle for heel is a much larger zone of 12 to 20 inches. I also expect the dog to stop when I stop, but not so instantly or precisely…as long as my leash never goes tight I'm usually satisfied. How strict you are is up to you.

Step into the heel position. Walk up to or step up to the side of your dog so the both of you are in the heel position. Reward Fido so that he will recognize this as the heel position. Pat the side of your leg, and you are now teaching a hand signal that will eventually be all that is required to get a "heel."

Now that you are both in the heel position, this will be the "official" start of your walk. Do not walk if the leash is tight (being pulled). Start with the leg that is on the same side as the dog, take one step, and stop (this will help Fido to notice when you start or stop). Repeat. Now take two steps and stop. Take one step and stop. Take two steps and stop. Try five steps and stop. Mix this exercise in randomly during the length of your walk, and heel for as long as you want.

If Fido is pulling on the leash, you will need to correct him. The following instructions are very specific and have never failed me. As soon as the leash gets tight, lean into it to create slack. Very quickly snap the leash backwards in line with the dog's back and only inches above it. This is not a "jerk" of the leash or a tug-of-war pulling match; it is similar to snapping a wet towel or throwing a dart or paper airplane.

You want the least amount of training or correction as possible. The very first time you do this you really need to make it count by using a lot of force and strength. This should last only a second. Do not choke your dog.

After the correction do not say anything. Stand still and turn your head away. Wait a few seconds then re-start the heel position ("step and stop" routines). If Fido continues to pull the leash, repeat the snap correction. Wait a few seconds and restart the heel position again. It may take ten minutes to walk ten feet. Walk only if your dog is politely walking beside you. I have not had to perform this correction more than twice. Dogs are very quick learners.

The correct heel position is critical for success. Your dog should see you at his side in order to read your cues about when to start and stop. Be aware that he can be slightly ahead of you and still see you beside him. (Dogs can see behind themselves.)

All your walks should mix in a little "dog" time. Within good judgment, let Fido do as he pleases part of the time.

— No matter where you are going
your dog wants to go —

Off Leash Heel

Once you have a good handle on the "come" command and have practiced heeling with a leash, you can begin heeling without the leash. Any time your dog runs free, be sure you are in a safe place. Never let your dog go as soon as you remove the leash; he should always continue "heeling" for a short period of time.

Start with letting the leash drop while "heeling." This way you can grab it or step on it if you need to send a message to your dog. Remove the leash according to your progress and confidence. Fold it in half and keep it visibly in your hand so your dog knows it's there. Perform the "heeling" instructions as you've done before. Occasionally have Fido return to you and attach the leash for more "on-leash heeling." Include free time, just as you have been doing. Ideally, "heeling" and "off-leash heeling" should end with an "OK" command for the dog to run about at will.

In summary, mix up interludes of on-leash heeling, off-leash heeling, and free running. You do not want your dog to think that the leash or the very act of heeling means the fun is over. This may lead to difficulties in coming when called.

— A dog always moves with
intent and objective —

Puppies

Training or conditioning your puppy starts from day one. The sooner you set standards for behaviour, the sooner you'll have a socially acceptable and enjoyable pet.

The following five items are all you will ever need to train a puppy:

    A 6-foot leash (to walk politely beside you)
    A 20-foot leash (teaches the subconscious 20 foot zone around you)
    A collar for tags
    A choker for training (when and if size permits)
    Toys (to amuse and interact with)

Never disturb your puppy when he is asleep or resting, unless necessary. A puppy grows rapidly, and what takes us about eighteen years, they do mostly in one year. While he is asleep or resting, he is also growing emotionally and physically. Before they reach six months of age, puppies are very receptive to suggestion and training. Puppies in competition rings win awards for obedience as early as ten to twelve weeks. The habits he develops now will guide him for the rest of his life. Everything in his life will influence his future behaviour. Be gentle, relaxed, understanding, and helpful; your dog wants to know what is good and bad.

A puppy's personality is contingent upon his environment. If two identical puppies are raised in two very different homes, one with five kids, two cats, a bird, a husband and a wife, and the other with a single, mature adult living in a quiet neighbourhood, it's quite obvious that these dogs will become very different animals. The busy family might put extra effort into making sure the puppy is getting the love, attention, and rest he needs. Or not. The single adult might diligently train the puppy, or perhaps he or she has an active social life and would have little time for a pet.

Dogs are creatures of habit; they generally like things to stay the same. Always try to maintain regularity for your dog, especially food times, bed, and morning times.

Just as you wouldn't let a barely-walking toddler wander around your house out of sight, try never to let your puppy out of sight. This will keep him safe and give you the time you need to study his developing habits and behaviour. If your puppy does something wrong, use your sub-sonic voice to "shame" him.

24 Hours to House Train (The Bathroom is Outside)

This technique has never failed me.

I'm going to ask you to make a one-day commitment and take your dog outside around the clock for twenty-four hours. Simply set your clock to sound an alarm every three hours. Always use the same door and always put your puppy down quickly in front of the door before you open it. Be sure to go outside early in the morning (seven or eight o'clock), after meals, after waking, after or during play, and before you go to bed at night. Begin with at least six times daily to start. It's not fair to expect a young puppy to "hold it" for eight hours or more, nor is it possible. Only when your dog's biology develops will he have the ability to hold it for long periods of time.

Do not end these outside trips too quickly after your dog does his "business." Dogs are smart and they like spending time outdoors. If you go back inside immediately, you may unintentionally teach him to lengthen the time outside.

This twenty-four-hour approach quickly creates a desire for your puppy to have a preference as to where to leave his mark. You have imprinted the pup's mind with a correlation between doing his business and the yard, grass, ground, whatever. After applying this routine, make sure you still provide many opportunities for the pup to be successful daily, as you want to avoid failure situations. In the beginning stages, you can let him walk out the door then carry him to his "spot." As he gets older you can simply direct him to his spot. If done correctly, your dog will remember which door leads to the great outdoors, he will go to that door, and he will wait for you or signal you when he needs to go out. You have now taught your dog to communicate his needs to you.

Building Confidence

If a two-year-old dog has been confined to a yard most of his life and then taken for a walk in a very public place with cars, people, buildings, trees, and other dogs or animals, this pooch will surely be a little confused and unsure of himself...he may even go berserk. A dog that has been frequently exposed to all kinds of environments and situations will be calm and well adjusted. Puppies learn and gain confidence through experience, so give your puppy the largest life possible. Take him with you as often as possible; even short drives to the store are great. Keep him guessing; keep him stimulated. Each trip or walk that ends safe and sound at home builds his confidence.

Mine/Yours

Have you ever told your teacher, *My dog ate my homework*? Or told your boss, *My dog ate my report*? Well, you'll never have to use this excuse again if you teach your puppy the difference between "mine" and "yours."

Everyone knows that babies explore their world by putting found objects in their mouths. A puppy is no different. This is a preventable behaviour addressed through the effort of constant observation. Snapping a quick "No!" corrects your pup when he picks up something he shouldn't or chews on something dangerous or of value. Your voice must express urgency. If you observe your dog about to pick something up, use your sub-sonic voice. (Further advice on this topic can be found in "Drop," below.)

Prevention is your aim. This is where a good variety and selection of toys comes in handy. Young dogs need something to chew and play with, preferably *not* your 100-page report or master's thesis. It's a natural part of learning and growing up. Make sure that every dog toy you purchase is safe. I also recommend choosing toys that do not resemble anything in the house, like an edible shoe toy or a fake newspaper roll. Dogs can be picky, so you may need to experiment with different textures: soft toys, rubber toys, squeakers, and chewables. Six to twenty toys are plenty.

Split the toys into two separate groups, alternating them daily. When you play with your pup, use all of them. Your dog will instigate his own interaction with these toys and at times will try to interest you in playtime. Aim to have some playtimes instigated by you and other times instigated by your dog. Have these playtimes two to six times a day. Your pup will quickly learn what is appropriate to chew on and play with.

"No" and "Drop"
(verbal command to release from mouth)

Although I've stressed the importance of preventative behaviour over correction, these two words are very important. They can save your puppy's life. There are other practical uses for these words, of course, but they are most beneficial for the safety of your dog.

NO

"No" is a little word with a lot of power. It has even more impact when it is unexpected; therefore, the best way to teach "no" is to startle your dog. Think of watching a scary movie, and at a very tense moment your friend suddenly grabs your arm! It doesn't hurt you at all, but it *really* gets your attention. Startling reaches your dog very deeply.

Most people startle their dogs the wrong way. They'll quickly rush over, usually shouting and yelling. The dog likely won't know what is going on, or why their owner is acting so crazy. There are too many signals at once. To correctly startle your dog, quietly sneak up on him and stamp your foot and clap your hands simultaneously, once. Then, in a loud, sharp voice, say, "No!" Do not scream at or strike your dog. You now have his full attention and the bad behaviour will have been prevented.

Drop

"Drop" is a universal term for getting a dog to release his grip. This is critical if your dog has picked up a dead animal or other nasty or dangerous item. Sometimes I use the word "out," but regardless of what word you choose, make sure it's one syllable and doesn't sound like one of the six other basic commands (sit, stay, down, come, heel, no). My dog, Chance, responds to "out" in many different ways: to release or "drop" an item, move out of my way, get out of or into the car, house, or a room.

The *tone* of your voice is significant here. It emphasizes the importance of *how* you say your commands more than *what* you say. Certainly your tone of voice will differ when your dog is playing frisbee or ball compared to when he is eating garbage or worse. Convey your message with the tone of your voice.

To teach your dog "drop," you will need an unfamiliar object. A new toy or two will suffice. Keeping your hand on the toy, allow Fido to take it in his mouth for one second. Take it back right away and say, "Drop!" at the same time. Sound authoritative. Try to do this ten times a day. Make Fido feel proud each and every time you get the toy back. Before the novelty of this toy has worn off, perhaps after two or five or twenty minutes, place your hand on the toy and say, "Drop." Wait one second and then take the toy swiftly; reward proudly. Remember to always have your hand on the toy before you command "drop." Do the same exercise with Fido's other toys over the next days and weeks.

The time you choose to practice these commands is critical. A dog park on a Saturday afternoon would not be recommended. Always make sure your dog is successful, and this involves carefully selecting lesson times.

If your dog does not release or drop then stop playing! The only attention your dog should get from you is when he releases properly. He may let you touch or hold the toy but won't release it. This isn't good enough. The first time you take it from him make sure he's rewarded, then toss it. Continue until your dog realizes how much more fun it is when he obeys drop.

— The dog is mentioned
14 times in the Bible—

Correction/Punishment

There are only two punishments I ever use:

A deep, low, slow voice. No shouting! Stretching out the words in this tone of voice acts as a warning to your dog. This affects him emotionally and "shames" him for his bad behaviour. He will know that you're disappointed in him.

A time-out. In the wild, dogs shun one another when they step out of line. This is not a lifelong punishment, rather a short, to-the-point message. You can do the same.

There are five steps to perform the time-out:

1) approach slowly;

2) gently grip the collar;

3) place the dog in the time-out zone
   (a bathroom or garage) and leave him by himself;

4) return thirty seconds later if all is quiet. Don't open the door if there is barking or scratching;

5) open the door to release the dog, saying nothing.
   If he is trying to bolt out the door, slow him down.

After he's out, he'll likely run to everyone in the house for some attention, but don't give in. Everyone should ignore him, and he'll likely go lie down. Call him a few minutes later; all's forgiven and forgotten.

If you find your dog in an unacceptable behaviour (like chewing your shoes) then you apply the quick, sharp "No." On the other hand if you catch your dog *about* to misbehave, then you apply the deep, low-slow voice to "warn"not to start that. The sharp-quick command implies an urgency to stop where as the low-slow command implies a warning to impending danger, before it gets started.

Why and How of Chokers

We humans need some way to connect with our dogs. If our arms were 10-20 feet long, then no leash or choker would be required. It is best used when teaching "anti-pull;" you certainly don't need one to sit, stay, down, or come.

I accept the use of a choker only when used correctly. It should never be used to actually choke! The choker works well because of the speed in which it can be applied and, more importantly, released. The proper correction should last one to two seconds; any longer and you are now playing a tug-of-war of choking! You only need to meet or slightly exceed the dog's power or force.

Always buy the highest quality, strongest, and smallest link speed choker available. Chrome or steel chokers are the strongest, but steel is the most expensive. Some may look like chrome or steel but are actually a white metal. Smaller links on the chain give quicker action, especially the "choker-release." Balance the strength and the link size relative to the size and strength of your dog to get both the strongest and quickest combination. (A small link choker is likely all that will ever be required). You should also have a comfortable collar.

Correct
Figure 1

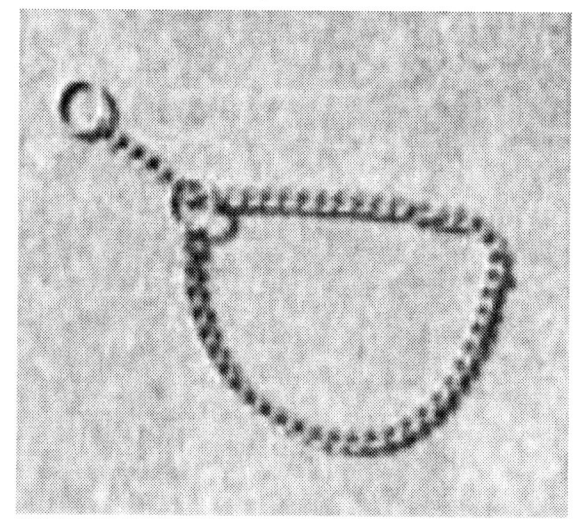

Incorrect
Figure 2

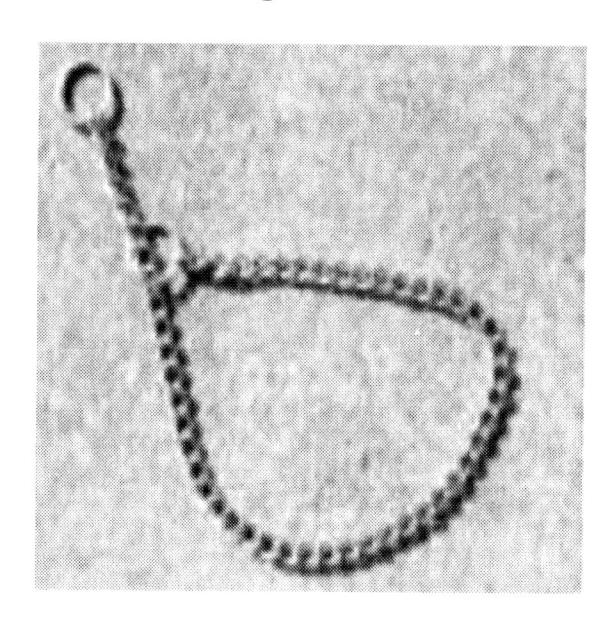

Protection Training

Are you a single woman? An elderly person living alone? Do you have a young family and live in a not-so-good neighbourhood? Are you in police or security work? Chances are if you have an interest in protection training, you have a large breed dog. Size alone often thwarts an intruder. Regardless of why you are interested in a dog for protection, you will find that not only will you get the feeling of security you desire, but you will also get a loving, warm companion as well. There is no reason that your protection dog can't be a docile house pet one minute and leap into protective action the next — should the need ever arise.

Dogs are den, cave or burrow-dwelling animals by nature. They will naturally protect their den (your house) with no training whatsoever! You are also the dog's care giver since you provide the food, shelter, and affection. You are the leader of the pack. A dog will naturally try to protect you!

There are three reactions a dog will naturally have if he feels threatened. First, he will sound the alarm by barking. Next he will either move towards the "bad guy" and possibly bite, or move away from the "bad guy" and threaten to bite. Either way, a dog will attempt to protect you to the best of his natural ability. Should a bad guy come into physical contact with you, most every dog will bite. However, even with a trained protection dog your safety is not guaranteed.

When dogs are trained for protection purposes only, they have to be subjected to negative emotional states like anger, contradicting their natural loving dispositions. To make your dog aggressive you would have to cause him physical pain and purposely aggravate him. Do you really want to do this? The best way to ensure that your pooch will protect you is love!

Build your dog's confidence in all areas of his life. Build his courage by providing lots of accomplishments. In other words, *bond* with your dog! The greater the bond, the greater potential he will give his life to protect you.

Dogs are like humans; we will always protect the ones we love! Just love the daylights out of your pet; the rest will come naturally.

Summary

In the simplest terms...let your dog be a dog! Include a one-second exercise every time you interact with your pooch. Many short one- to five-second "commands" throughout the day and week create a solid foundation for continual success.

As your dog grows, his natural maturity blossoms. Fido is learning not only specific techniques but also the overall philosophy and understanding of being loved and cherished for proper behaviour (and even misbehaviour). Never stop observing your dog. There are always opportunities for one-second training.

The four key ways and other instructions in this book work together to build a better pooch. Pin the "Top Twelve Rules" on the fridge for all to see. Have a meeting of the minds if more than one person is involved in training. If you've learned that you've contributed to some of the bad behaviour in your pup or dog, then I have two words that are guaranteed to work: "STOP IT." Study yourself and your family, your dog, his day, and this book, and you will notice a difference in the next twenty-four hours. You will continue to create the best dog you can, every day, second by second.

Kevin Meehan
The Dog Tutor

"Dog spelled backwards is God."
— Author Unknown

Printed in the United States
35554LVS00007B/169-261